RATE
YOURSELF!

RATE
YOURSELF!

ASSESS YOUR **SKILLS,**
PERSONALITY AND
ABILITIES FOR THE
JOB YOU WANT

MARTHE SANSREGRET AND DYANE ADAMS

KOGAN
PAGE

YOURS TO HAVE AND TO HOLD

BUT NOT TO COPY

First published in 1997 as *My Transferable Skills Checklist Plus My Personality Traits* by Éditions Hurtubise HMH Itée, Canada

Edited and revised by Karen Henchey

This edition published in 1998 by Kogan Page

Kogan Page Limited
120 Pentonville Road
London N1 9JN

© Éditions Hurtubise HMH Itée 1997, 1998

British Library Cataloguing in Publication Data

A CIP record for this book is available from the British Library.

ISBN 0 7494 2597 0

Typeset by Kogan Page
Printed and bound in Great Britain by Clays Ltd, St Ives plc

Contents

Acknowledgements

We wish to sincerely thank the members of the steering committee for the inestimable amount of time, energy and enthusiasm they have devoted to this project and for their highly-valued competence:

Colette Arsenault
Action-Éducation-Femmes, réseau national

Margot Cardinal
Collectif des femmes francophones du Nord-Est ontarien
Action-Éducation-Femmes, Ontario

Nicole Cholette
Centre ÉTAPE

Catherine Demers
Ontario Women's Directorate

Louise Gervais
Collectif des femmes francophones du Nord-Est ontarien

Rolande Savoie
Action-Éducation-Femmes, réseau national, projet
Alphabétisation

We would also like to express our gratitude to all who contributed to the success of this project by reviewing the manuscript and providing valuable feedback. Finally, we would like to especially acknowledge the warm support we received from the faculty, administration and students of Boréal College in Sudbury, Ontario.

Welcome!

Today's world of work is anything but tranquil – people often find themselves tossed about by new circumstances and unexpected obstacles.

Imagine this: You arrive for work one morning only to find out that you will not be returning the following day. What has happened? Unfortunately, your job has been cut. You have to pick yourself up, brush yourself off, and start looking for another job.

If you are a recent graduate, a newly-arrived immigrant, or someone who has not worked outside the home for a number of years, it is very possible that you are beginning your search for paid employment with some trepidation. Your self-confidence may not be what it should be.

Nonetheless, you may be saying to yourself: 'But I know I can do a lot of things!' For example, you enjoy talking to people, reading newspapers and books, and writing. You are comfortable in the company of others and are very interested in computers. You do not shy away from physical activity, and you enjoy doing odd jobs around your home.

Perhaps you possess a good deal of artistic talent. You know how to co-ordinate colours, you appreciate great cooking, and you enjoy listening to music. You are very good at managing your personal finances, and sometimes you even help others create budgets of their own.

Perhaps you are the one that others always rely on to carefully plan, organize and co-ordinate family reunions and community events. Whenever a problem comes up, people know they can count on you to think creatively and find a solution. Maybe you are someone who has already started your own small business or are on the verge of doing so.

When you think about it, then, you come to the conclusion that you do indeed have many skills and abilities. Regardless of when or where you acquired these skills and abilities, they share a common characteristic: **they are transferable.** That is, they can be used again in another context, **in a paying job,** for instance.

So you do have a lot to offer a potential employer after all. You cannot, however, expect employers or organizations that lend money to small businesses to automatically know that you have these skills to offer.

If you are presently searching for a job, if you believe that the moment has come to ask for a promotion, or if you simply desire to create an accurate inventory of your skills for your own personal interest, then you will certainly find this book useful.

The book's primary goal is to help you to **name** and **classify** all the skills you believe you have developed at one time or other in your life that you can use again in a different context – particularly in the world of work.

The book is divided into a series of questionnaires. There is a questionnaire for each of the following categories: communication (verbal and nonverbal communication, reading and writing); inter-personal relations; computer skills; physical abilities and manual skills; artistic expression; financial management; planning and or-ganizing; and problem solving. The ninth questionnaire, which is called 'Entrepreneurship,' is sure to interest you if you are planning to start your own business. Whether you decide to look for a job with a company or create a small business of your own, it is important for you to review your *personality traits*. This is the subject of the special tenth questionnaire of the book.

Once you have completed all 10 questionnaires, you are ready to do the very final questionnaire. This questionnaire **reviews** your strengths and weaknesses in all 10 areas, allowing you to get a global view of your skills and capabilities. This self-knowledge is extremely valuable. It allows you to confidently write of your abilities in a formal letter to a potential employer or lending organization, in an employment application, in a curriculum vitae, in your 'portfolio,' or speak about them during a job interview.

Before you begin, please read the instructions that follow. They describe the best way to work through the questionnaires in this book.

How to use this book

You will complete nine checklists that will enable you to identify and classify your skills and abilities and a special tenth checklist that will allow you to identify your personality traits. You can start with the first checklist, which corresponds to the first category (it's the longest questionnaire), or you can begin with another checklist. In other words, you do not have to complete the checklists in the order they are given. The procedure you must follow is always the same, though, and it is described below.

- **Read** the short preamble that precedes the checklist. The preamble is designed to divert your attention away from your current thoughts and preoccupations and get you thinking about the topic that will be explored in the checklist.

- Then **read** the definition of the category you are about to explore.

- **Review** the scale you will use to describe the level of your skills and abilities:

  ***** = Excellent
  **** = Very Good
  *** = Good
  ** = Fair
  ֠ * = None

- **Read** each question and **put a tick** in the appropriate column. It is better to use a pencil when completing the questionnaires because you may want to go back and change evaluations you made earlier.

Here is an example of what a completed questionnaire looks like:

4

▶ DISCOVERING MY VERBAL AND NONVERBAL COMMUNICATION SKILLS

AT WHAT LEVEL AM I ABLE TO...
communicate effectively?

	*** **	** **	** *	**	*
▶ I AM AT EASE communicating					
● at home	✓				
– with my partner	✓				
– with my children	✓				
– with my parents		✓			
● in society					
– with my neighbours		✓			
– with suppliers			✓		
– with people I meet for the first time		✓			
– with other employees		✓			
▶ I CAN choose the right words					
● name an object correctly		✓			
● describe a situation with accuracy				✓	
● use the appropriate vocabulary					✓

Try to be as objective as possible when you fill in the checklists. For example, if you genuinely believe that your skills in a specific area are 'Excellent,' put a tick in that column; if you believe your skills are slightly less than excellent, put a tick in the next column and so on. If you honestly believe that you do not possess any skills in a specific area, do not hesitate to put a tick in the 'None' column. But please do not judge yourself too harshly! For example, do not put yourself in the 'Good' column when you know that you actually do better than 'Good.'

5

You will complete the final review checklist the same way you completed the first 10. For each question, you will **put a tick** in the appropriate column.

Have fun!

Category 1

Communication (verbal and nonverbal communication, reading, writing)

‘*O*h, *you just don't understand!' she says to him in exasperation.*

Why did they argue that morning? Was it because they awoke to the sound of rain and the distant rumblings of thunder? Two people, though in love, complain about their lack of communication. Their dissatisfaction shows that it is not always easy for people to express themselves – even those who have chosen to share their lives 'for better or for worse'.

Many years ago, before the invention of the telephone, people sent letters to declare their love for another. Sometimes these love letters were delivered by the letter writer; other times, by a messenger on foot or horseback. Because it took time for the letter to reach its destination, the recipient had ample time to think, to imagine, to wonder... Today, everything happens at lightning speed. In consequence, that interval of time, which gave people the leisure to wonder and speculate, has disappeared. And the letter carrier of today is more likely to bring bills, not tender words of love...

In our modern world, written messages are rapidly dispatched by e-mail and received within seconds. People take a cursory look at the messages they send, hoping that their choice of words was appropriate and that they wrote just enough to accurately transmit their messages. Usually the messages deal with work-related topics, although once in a while they may convey heart-felt emotions.

Whether they are misunderstood lovers or dissatisfied employers, people today complain about the poor quality of communication. Teachers are often held responsible for this problem. Now imagine this: A group of teachers have decided to act on the problem—it's now or never. They are holding a contest. The goal of the contest: to stimulate adults and young adults to show their accomplishments as communicators. The contest has three categories: verbal and non-verbal communication, reading, and writing.

The contest is about to begin and you are one of the participants. Your goal: to find and classify your abilities in these three areas of communication. Be sure to give yourself the opportunity to explore your thoughts and express your opinions...

Definition

Competence in verbal and nonverbal communication, reading, and writing means having acquired knowledge and knowing what to do and how to be so that you can exchange, learn and transmit information, ideas, messages, opinions, news, etc. As a competent communicator, you convey your message sometimes through gestures, sometimes through spoken words, and sometimes through written words. You do so in your native tongue and possibly in other languages as well.

▶ DISCOVERING MY VERBAL AND NONVERBAL COMMUNICATION SKILLS

AT WHAT LEVEL AM I ABLE TO...
communicate effectively?

	*** / **	** / **	** / *	**	*
▶ I AM AT EASE communicating					
● at home					
– with my partner					
– with my children					
– with my parents					
● in society					
– with my neighbours					
– with people I meet for the first time					
– with people from different origins and ethnic backgrounds					
– with suppliers					
– with employers					
– with my co-workers					
– with other employees					
▶ I CAN choose the right words					
● name an object correctly					
● describe a situation with accuracy					
● use the appropriate vocabulary					
▶ I CAN speak clearly					
● pronounce words correctly					
● control my voice and emotions					
● speak clearly on the telephone					

*** / ** = Excellent   ** / ** = Very Good   ** / * = Good   ** = Fair   * = None

	*** **	** **	** *	**	*

▶ *I CAN keep up a conversation*
- look directly at the other person
- reformulate a question in my own words
- keep to the subject of the conversation
- initiate a dialogue and keep it going

▶ *I CAN make myself understood*
- use gestures
- express my needs, wishes, opinions
- reformulate in my own words the opinions and ideas expressed by others

▶ *I CAN have interesting ideas*
- see things from different angles; imagine different possibilities
- think of solutions
- inspire others

▶ *I CAN talk about a variety of subjects*
- explain my views on business and economics
- interpret a work of art
- analyse the current state of education
- educate others about the environment
- interpret nutrition guidelines

*** ** = Excellent   ** ** = Very Good   ** * = Good   ** = Fair   * = None

	*** **	** **	** *	**	*
• describe the geography of different locations					
• comment on historical events					
• give my opinion on fashion trends					
• talk about music					
• comment on political events					
• discuss aptitudes and behaviours					
• interpret the message of an advertisement					
• discuss religious faith and practices					
• follow developments in scientific or medical research					
• comment on the relations between different peoples					
• comment on sports events					
• give an account of my travels					

*** ** = Excellent   ** ** = Very Good   ** * = Good   ** = Fair   * = None

11

AT WHAT LEVEL AM I ABLE TO...
communicate in public?

	$\overset{***}{**}$	$\overset{**}{**}$	$\overset{**}{*}$	$**$	$*$
▶ *I CAN participate in a meeting, round-table discussion, conference*					
● overcome the fear of public speaking					
● express my point of view					
● listen to the opinions of others					
▶ *I CAN lead a group discussion*					
● choose a method to lead the discussion					
● follow the progress of the discussion on a flip chart or blackboard					
● encourage others to participate					
● ensure that the opinions of others are respected					
● reconcile different points of view					
● maintain the group's interest					
▶ *I CAN make an effective presentation*					
● give a short talk					
● use acetates, slides, and videos and discuss their contents					
● use humour to enliven a topic					
● maintain the group's interest					
● use a microphone					
● use a flip chart or blackboard to summarize different points					
● keep within the allotted time frame					
● close the presentation and thank all participants					

$\overset{***}{**}$ = Excellent $\overset{**}{**}$ = Very Good $\overset{**}{*}$ = Good $**$ = Fair $*$ = None

	*** **	** **	** *	**	*
▶ *I CAN respond to questions from the media (newspaper, radio, television)*					
• overcome the fear of public speaking					
• control my voice and breathing					
• keep to the subject at hand					

▶ DISCOVERING MY READING SKILLS

AT WHAT LEVEL AM I ABLE TO...
read effectively?

	*** **	** **	** *	**	*
▶ *I CAN focus on what I am reading*					
• think about the subject in depth					
• retain the important information					
▶ *I CAN read rapidly and intelligently*					
• read quickly through a text and persevere until the end					

 = Excellent   ** ** = Very Good   ** * = Good   ** = Fair   * = None

Rate Yourself!

	*** **	** **	** *	**	*

- get a general idea of the topic dealt with
- get the essential meaning
- classify the information in a logical way

▶ *I CAN use reference material*
- find the information I need
- consult a grammar book
- consult dictionaries, indexes, and lexicons
- consult encyclopedias
- interpret tables and statistics

AT WHAT LEVEL AM I ABLE TO...
read different types of material on different subjects?

	*** **	** **	** *	**	*

▶ *I CAN understand certain types of documents*
- understand the questions in a questionnaire
- verify the information given in bills, receipts, purchase orders

▶ *I CAN understand different types of reading material*
- decipher the information given on tickets, notes, etc

*** ** = Excellent   ** ** = Very Good   ** * = Good   ** = Fair   * = None

14

	$***$ $**$	$**$ $**$	$**$ $*$	$**$	$*$

- interpret classified ads, print advertising
- follow instructions, directions, recipes
- get the essence of a news item or fact
- comment on and understand the essence of a text
- read different types of writing (biographies, fiction, stories, editorials, reports, etc.)

▶ *I CAN interpret the contents of different types of letters*
- personal letters
- thank-you notes
- letters conveying congratulations, condolences
- letters expressing a complaint
- letters requesting information
- letters requesting employment or announcing an offer of service
- letters of resignation, letters notifying of the cancellation of a contract

▶ *I CAN understand a formal or legal document*
- interpret an offer of purchase or sale
- understand different safety rules (fire and theft prevention, the rules of the road, etc.)

$***$ $**$ = Excellent $**$ $**$ = Very Good $**$ $*$ = Good $**$ = Fair $*$ = None

	*** **	** **	** *	**	*

- respect an agenda
- interpret a report
- interpret minutes/proceedings
- understand the differences between report cards, certificates, diplomas, etc.
- understand the meaning of medical prescriptions and reports
- interpret a collective agreement
- interpret a judgment rendered by a court of law

▶ *I CAN study written works at length*
- choose serious, reliable authors
- analyse, comment on, compare the works of different authors
- imagine the people, places and circumstances of a novel
- criticize a text objectively
- follow a historical narrative, a travel narrative, etc.
- interpret a humorous text
- comment on a biography

*** ** = Excellent   ** ** = Very Good   ** * = Good   ** = Fair   * = None

▶ DISCOVERING MY WRITING SKILLS

AT WHAT LEVEL AM I ABLE TO...
write effectively?

	*** **	** **	** *	**	*
▶ I CAN reflect on the subject before beginning to write					
• summarize my thoughts clearly					
• make notes					
▶ I CAN write easily and rapidly					
• find the right words					
• organize my thoughts					
• present my thoughts in clear sentences					
▶ I CAN write a clear text					
• construct a sentence, paragraph, an entire text					
• apply the rules of good grammar					
– use appropriate verbs, adjectives, adverbs, etc.					
– use correct punctuation					
• follow the correct format for a research paper					
– give accurate references					
– create a table of contents					
– create a bibliography					

*** ** = Excellent   ** ** = Very Good   ** * = Good   ** = Fair   * = None

AT WHAT LEVEL AM I ABLE TO...
write in different styles?

	*** **	** **	** *	**	*
▶ *I CAN complete certain types of documents*					
● fill in information on a form/questionnaire					
● fill in an invoice, receipt, purchase order					
▶ *I CAN write different types of documents*					
● write a memo					
● write the text for a classified ad					
● write out instructions, directions, recipes					
● write an objective summary of a news item or event					
● analyse and summarize a text					
● write about my own life and experiences (autobiography)					
● create a fictional text					
▶ *I CAN write different types of letters*					
● write personal letters					
● write thank-you letters					
● write letters conveying congratulations, condolences					
● write letters expressing a complaint					
● write letters requesting information					

*** ** = Excellent   ** ** = Very Good   ** * = Good   ** = Fair   * = None

18

	*** **	** **	** *	**	*

- write letters requesting employment or announcing an offer of service
- write letters of resignation or letters notifying of the cancellation of a contract

▶ *I CAN write a formal/legal document*
- write the agenda for a meeting
- write a report
- write the minutes/proceedings of a meeting
- write an offer of purchase or sale

*** ** = Excellent   ** ** = Very Good   ** * = Good   ** = Fair   * = None

Category 2

Interpersonal relations

*I*t has often been said that our world is getting smaller and smaller.

Information transmitted via satellite connects people all over the world so quickly that we sometimes have difficulty imagining the actual distances that separate us. Modern means of transportation allow us to travel very far in a very short period of time so that it is indeed possible to eat your breakfast at home and your lunch in some far-off place thousands of kilometres away... We really do live in a 'global village,' as the celebrated author Marshall McLuhan once wrote.

Imagine this situation. A group of strangers are gathered together in an airport departure lounge in eager anticipation. They are *all the lucky winners of a two-week whirlwind tour of our global village with stopovers in a number of interesting and exotic locations.*

There is joy in the air. The travellers are happy to leave their cares and worries for a couple of weeks. No going to work, no having to deal with the small problems that come up in daily life, and, yes, the opportunity to get away from the disagreeable people in their lives... Does life get any better than this?

But, alas, the joy and levity does not last. A few hours into the voyage, the atmosphere on the plane starts to change. The problem is not a mechanical one, but a human one. Certain passengers have started to feel grumpy and peevish and they are making sure all their fellow passengers are aware of this. They are the sort of people who—regardless of where they are or what they are doing—seem quite content to spoil the happiness of others, so long as their own moods and feelings are addressed. Although barely perceptible at first, this unfortunate change in the plane's atmosphere becomes all too obvious to everyone on the flight.

It is in this casual way that the interpersonal-relations game begins. How will the easy-going passengers deal with their less agreeable fellow travellers? All of this will happen under the watchful eyes of the flight crew, who are, of course, expert players of the interpersonal-relations game.

How did the dream trip turn out? The travellers have not yet returned to tell their stories. But there is nothing to stop us from guessing...

Definition

Competence in interpersonal relations means having acquired knowledge and knowing what to do and how to be so that you can develop and maintain satisfying relationships with others.

▶ DISCOVERING MY COMPETENCE IN INTERPERSONAL RELATIONS

AT WHAT LEVEL AM I ABLE TO...
develop and maintain good and effective interpersonal relations?

	*** **	** **	** *	**	*
▶ I CAN create an agreeable and stimulating atmosphere					
● know myself and accept myself as I am					
● be at ease with others					
● understand that other people are important					
▶ I CAN collaborate with others					
● express my point of view clearly and listen to the opinions expressed by others					
● use convincing arguments					
● appreciate the value of the efforts and merits of others					
● thank others with sincerity					
▶ I CAN make commitments and keep them					
● clarify the nature of my commitments					
● live up to my commitments to the best of my ability					
● keep my word					

*** ** = Excellent   ** ** = Very Good   ** * = Good   ** = Fair   * = None

23

*** **	** **	** *	**	*

▶ *I CAN objectively re-evaluate my attitudes and behaviour*
  ● analyse a situation calmly
  ● make the necessary adjustments

AT WHAT LEVEL AM I ABLE TO...
develop and maintain interpersonal relations at work and in social and community activities?

*** **	** **	** *	**	*

▶ *I CAN work as part of a team*
  ● take part in committees
  ● work alongside people with different backgrounds (with respect to age, culture, economic status, religion, ethnic origin)

*** ** = Excellent   ** ** = Very Good   ** * = Good   ** = Fair   * = None

	*** **	** **	** *	**	*

- accept interpersonal differences
- learn to acknowledge different interests
- provide support to the other members of the group
- try to understand a difficult situation
- comfort and support members of the group who are having trouble
- show courtesy to others

▶ *I CAN work in partnerships (collaborations with people, groups, companies)*

- collaborate to establish common goals
- define my responsibilities
- interpret a partnership agreement
- share my knowledge and information
- respect confidentiality
- work irregular hours if necessary (days, evenings, every day, shared time)
- work in different locations (at home, outside the home, in a foreign country)

*** ** = Excellent   ** ** = Very Good   ** * = Good   ** = Fair   * = None

AT WHAT LEVEL AM I ABLE TO...
develop and maintain interpersonal relations when I am in a leadership role?

	***** (★★★★★)	**** (★★★★)	*** (★★★)	**	*

▶ *I CAN take initiative*
- define and explain duties and responsibilities
- focus on the objectives and keep to them

▶ *I CAN create a favourable climate for collaboration*
- encourage autonomy and initiative in others
- define and clearly explain the duties and responsibilities of each team member
- stimulate and motivate the group
- keep the group informed and guide the members to a common objective
- remain open to the needs and opinions of the members

▶ *I CAN sense power conflicts*
- reduce the tension
- help to reach a compromise
- act according to my conscience and make realistic decisions

▶ *I CAN evaluate my leadership skills*
- review the results obtained to ensure that the group's objectives are met

*** / ** = Excellent   ** / ** = Very Good   *** = Good   ** = Fair   * = None

26

*** **	** **	** *	**	*

- determine what improvements need to be made
- prepare for a change-over of leaders
- withdraw when the time is right

*** ** = Excellent   ** ** = Very Good   ** * = Good   ** = Fair   * = None

Category 3

Computer skills

*T*he days when the manual typewriter was the most modern piece
of office equipment are long since past. This trusted companion
of secretaries, journalists, and two-finger-typing students alike was
replaced in the 1950s by the electric typewriter. And what a marvel
that was—a carriage return at the mere press of a button!

But the electric typewriter was only the beginning. We all know
how electronic equipment, always magical and fascinating, has
changed the way we work and live. Computers are everywhere. They
make it possible to accomplish many tasks more quickly and easily.
At the supermarket, cashiers use optical scanners that allow them to
register the items and automatically deduct them from the store's
inventory. Customers pay for their purchases with debit cards that

*automatically deduct the amounts from their bank balances. In the home, more and more parents are using computers, that is, when they can pry them away from their children. And one nagging question remains in the minds of the parents: 'Are the kids **really** doing their homework or are they surfing the Net again?'*

Computers have created a large number of new interests. For some, machines and electronic gadgets have become a passion. But what particular skills does a person need to have in order to use a computer competently?

Definition

Competence in computers means having acquired knowledge and knowing what to do and how to be so that you can do the following: write and edit documents, make calculations, communicate with others, analyse information, create an inventory or directory, catalogue information, process data, and create tables and graphs. All this is accomplished with the aid of a computer equipped with the necessary programs and applications.

▶ DISCOVERING MY COMPETENCE WITH COMPUTERS

AT WHAT LEVEL AM I ABLE TO...
use computers effectively on the job?

	*** / **	** / **	** / *	**	*
▶ I AM ABLE TO					
• determine the conditions that create a favourable work environment					
• (lighting, furniture, break time, etc.)					
• follow a basic course on computers					
• use reference manuals					
▶ I CAN work quickly					
• touch-type at a rapid pace					
• find the information I need in computer manuals quickly					
• learn different computer programs quickly					
▶ I CAN explain the uses of different modern technologies (fax machines, computerized cash registers, computers, printers, modems, etc.)					
• understand different modern technologies and their uses					
• distinguish between different computer programs and their applications					

*** / ** = Excellent   ** / ** = Very Good   ** / * = Good   ** = Fair   * = None

AT WHAT LEVEL AM I ABLE TO...
master different ways of using computers?

	***/**	**/**	**/*	**	*
▶ I CAN use a word-processing program and printer					
● install the program					
● design a page layout and choose appropriate typefaces					
● create tables					
● teach word processing to others					
● edit a text					
● give advice on the subject					
▶ I CAN create a database					
● gather the data					
● create files					
● update the files					
● teach others how to create and use databases					
● give advice on the subject					

***/** = Excellent   **/** = Very Good   **/* = Good   ** = Fair   * = None

	$\substack{*** \\ **}$	$\substack{** \\ **}$	$\substack{** \\ *}$	**	*

▶ *I CAN connect with a network or the Internet*
- open myself to the world
- understand the Internet: how it works, its scope, its implications
- make links with others interested in the same subjects through bulletin boards, web sites
- find out about the constraints of a network (ways to collaborate, work agendas, etc.)
- exchange, select, and share information
- accept different approaches, viewpoints, cultures, etc.
- give advice on the subject

▶ *I CAN create and analyse programs*
- study the subject to be programmed
- think about the goals of the program
- imagine the concept to be programmed
- forecast the steps required to develop the concept
- develop and improve programs
- teach others how to create and analyse programs
- give advice related to creating and analysing programs

$\substack{*** \\ **}$ = Excellent $\substack{** \\ **}$ = Very Good $\substack{** \\ *}$ = Good   ** = Fair   * = None

Category 4

Physical abilities and manual skills

*I*t really is quite something to watch... Have you ever seen the extreme care normally clumsy people can use when manipulating such precious objects as their sound systems and CDs? But will this delicacy of movement be in evidence when these same people venture onto the dance floor? Easy does it... pay attention to the rhythm and pace of the music, execute the appropriate steps, and watch out for unforeseen obstacles – like feet!

When you think about it, our bodies perform a wide variety of physical tasks each day. On a typical day, you may find yourself moving furniture to access an electric outlet, running up and down the stairs countless times, repairing a bicycle to stop that annoying *squeak, stirring a sauce on the stove so that it will not boil over, sewing a button without pricking a finger and on it goes.*

And think of all the times your physical exertions really made a difference, like the time when you repaired the break in the upstairs pipe before the entire bathroom could come crashing down into the kitchen or the time when you sprinted across the street and snatched a neighbour's child from the path of a speeding car.

So off you go on your morning jog... After all, you need to be in shape for the next physical challenge to come your way.

Definition

Physical and manual competence means having acquired knowledge and knowing what to do and how to be so that you can make effective movements and gestures and deploy your manual skills in different activities.

▶ DISCOVERING MY PHYSICAL ABILITIES

AT WHAT LEVEL AM I ABLE TO...
make effective movements
and gestures?

	*** **	** **	** *	**	*

▶ *I CAN keep myself in good physical condition*
- move with suppleness and agility
- remain in the same position for a long time
- climb up and down stairs without getting breathless
- walk for long periods of time
- have good reflexes

▶ *I CAN show endurance*
- run without getting breathless
- strengthen myself through sports and exercise
- make a sustained physical effort

▶ *I CAN use my physical strength*
- move heavy objects
- lift heavy weights
- push and pull objects

*** ** = Excellent　** ** = Very Good　** * = Good　** = Fair　* = None

AT WHAT LEVEL
AM I ABLE TO...
make effective
movements and
gestures in different
types of activities?

	*** **	** **	** *	**	*
▶ I CAN maintain my equilibrium					
• climb a step ladder, an extension ladder, on a roof					
• jump for a while without stumbling					
▶ I CAN make an effort requiring continuous rhythmic movement					
• walk quickly					
• run long distances					
• jump over obstacles					
• cycle long distances					
• swim a fair distance					

*** = Excellent   ** = Very Good   ** = Good   ** = Fair   * = None
 **   **   *

38

▶ DISCOVERING MY MANUAL SKILLS

AT WHAT LEVEL AM I ABLE TO...
demonstrate my manual skills effectively?

	*** **	** **	** *	**	*
▶ I CAN perform basic manual tasks					
● knot, attach, twist ropes, thread, etc.					
● manipulate small objects with dexterity					
● make electrical and mechanical appliances and plumbing devices work according to safety standards					
▶ I CAN perform manual tasks in the kitchen					
● cut and chop food					
● mix liquids and solids					
● knead and roll out pastry					
● cut up meat					
● thicken a sauce					
▶ I CAN perform diverse manual tasks					
● feel, turn, and level different materials					
● cut out, tailor, and sew items, using different types of fabric					
● differentiate among different textures, surfaces, shapes, lengths, thicknesses					
● convey messages or orders using finger or hand gestures					

*** ** = Excellent   ** ** = Very Good   ** * = Good   ** = Fair   * = None

AT WHAT LEVEL AM I ABLE TO...
demonstrate my manual skills in
different contexts?

	*****	****	***	**	*

▶ ***I CAN use different instruments
and materials to create objects and
clothing***
  - operate a sewing machine
  - use knitting needles and crochet hooks
  - use an embroidery hoop, canvas
  - prepare a loom and weave

▶ ***I CAN use different household and
gardening tools***
  - sow seeds and cultivate a vegetable garden
  - plant and cultivate exterior plants, shrubs, and trees
  - look after the grounds
  - do odd jobs inside and outside the home
  - assemble furniture
  - paint flat and jagged surfaces
  - wallpaper walls
  - refinish furniture
  - perform different operations, including cutting, cutting out, hammering, sanding, polishing, varnishing, countersinking a screw/bolt
  - repair objects, furniture

***** = Excellent   *** = Very Good   *** = Good   ** = Fair   * = None

	$\overset{***}{**}$	$\overset{**}{**}$	$\overset{**}{*}$	**	*

▶ *I CAN work different materials*
- sculpt wood
- work metal
- engrave stone

▶ *I CAN install and make different electrical and electronic appliances work*
- install a sound system, videocassette recorder, fax machine by following the manufacturer's instructions
- link up a computer, printer, modem
- install an antenna

▶ *I CAN assemble different things*
- set up a tent, camping equipment, etc.
- build a fire in a fireplace or at a campsite and maintain it
- put up a fence, shed, etc.
- construct a building according to the building code

▶ *I CAN drive different types of vehicles and obey the rules of the road and all safety regulations*
- ride a bicycle well
- drive a car well
- drive a truck or lorry well

$\overset{***}{**}$ = Excellent $\overset{**}{**}$ = Very Good $\overset{**}{*}$ = Good   ** = Fair   * = None

Category 5

Artistic expression

A large company is preparing to celebrate its fiftieth anniversary. *On this occasion, the company has chosen quite a novel way to thank its employees.*

According to a recent survey, only seven percent of the employees know who is who and who does what within the company. To help remedy this situation, an entire week of festivities is planned. During that week, people will get an opportunity to introduce themselves and describe the work they do to their fellow employees **using their own particular artistic talents.** And given the multicultural nature of the *employee population, the festivities are sure to be a fascinating display.*

An unusual call for tenders begins to appear on bulletin boards throughout the company. It stipulates the following: 'Spouses of company employees are also invited to showcase their artistic talents' and 'A budget will be allotted to each participant to cover the cost of materials and equipment rentals for the activity he or she has chosen.'

A co-ordinating committee is set up to organize the celebrations, which will take place in six months. Because the employees know little about one another, the number of hidden talents waiting to be displayed astounds everyone. All shyness forgotten, a whopping ninety-three percent of the employees respond to the call, and this is not counting the impressive number of responses received from spouses!

But wait a minute: Who was it that said that questions of taste and colour cannot be discussed?

Definition

Artistic competence means having acquired knowledge and knowing what to do and how to be so that you can express yourself, innovate, create, relax and inspire and delight others through taste, sound, smell, colour, shape, touch, and movement.

▶ DISCOVERING MY COMPETENCE IN ARTISTIC EXPRESSION

AT WHAT LEVEL AM I ABLE TO...
use my artistic talents effectively?

	*** **	** **	** *	**	*
▶ I CAN stimulate my own creativity					
• dream, give free rein to my imagination					
• allow myself to make mistakes					
• live with doubt, uncertainty					
▶ I CAN use my five senses					
• taste different foods and appreciate their flavours					
• hear and differentiate noises and sounds and find their origin					
• smell the nuances of different scents and odours					
• see and distinguish the differences and harmony between colours					
• touch and distinguish between different textures and shapes					

*** = Excellent   ** = Very Good   ** = Good   ** = Fair   * = None
**   **   *

AT WHAT LEVEL AM I ABLE TO...
use my artistic talents in different activities that involve...

	*** **	** **	** *	**	*

▶ *Using my sense of taste*
  - try different foods
  - select foods for their flavour and freshness
  - season foods
  - prepare exotic meals
  - sample and select wines according to their characteristics, age, and the foods they will accompany

▶ *Using my sense of hearing*
  - distinguish between different noises and sounds and find their origin
  - play a musical instrument
  - use music to express myself
  - compose a piece of music
  - sight-read music while playing an instrument

▶ *Using my sense of smell*
  - detect different smells and odours
  - create a pleasant atmosphere through cooking smells, flower scents, aromatic oils (potpourris), incense, etc.

*** ** = Excellent   ** ** = Very Good   ** * = Good   ** = Fair   * = None

	*** **	** **	** *	**	*

▶ *Using my sense of sight*
- differentiate between colours and their intensities, and be able to harmonize them
- appreciate the nature of different shapes (long and short, round and flat, square and rectangular, oblong, etc.)
- think up a decorating scheme and create comfortable and aesthetic interiors (furniture, accessories, etc.)
- fix up an exterior (equipment, flowers, shrubs, etc.)
- create effects with light and shadow
- photograph scenes from interesting angles
- make sketches, draw people, landscapes, still lifes, etc., using a variety of techniques (pastels, watercolours, etc.)
- analyse photos, drawings, paintings, etc.

▶ *Using my sense of touch and movement and dexterity*
- differentiate between textures (smooth and rough, soft and hard, etc.)
- understand the properties of different materials (wood, metal, stone, etc.)
- dance to music with grace and suppleness
- act in a play

***
** = Excellent **
** = Very Good **
* = Good ** = Fair * = None

Category 6

Financial management

*I*n these tough economic times, we would all love to be able to buy the best quality item at the lowest possible price and not have to pay a pence until January 2002!

Because jobs seem less and less secure these days, it is important to be economical. But, then again, life is short—so why not enjoy ourselves now, while we can?

Many of us find ourselves thinking these contradictory thoughts. We hesitate between the necessity of economizing, of planning for the long term, and the desire to purchase additional goods and services that will make our lives more enjoyable right now.

One morning, you awake thinking how wonderful it would be to have a small home of your own on a bit of land located close to schools and shops in a quiet neighbourhood. Why not a small vegetable patch in the back garden as well?

You find yourself thinking about this dream of owning your own home more and more each day. Could it become a reality? You start to notice the 'For Sale' signs and each house seems more interesting than the last. They all stand in wait, ready to fulfil your dream. You begin to lose sleep over this cherished dream of yours – so anxious are you to see it become a reality.

But before you can realize your dream, you have to consider how you are going to manage your finances. Who knows? Maybe you will discover a hidden talent in this area. And maybe you will be crunching into your home-grown organic vegetables sooner than you think...

Definition

Competence in financial management means having acquired knowledge and knowing what to do and how to be that allows you to establish a base from which you can control your expenses and revenues over a given period of time.

▶ DISCOVERING MY COMPETENCE IN FINANCIAL MANAGEMENT

AT WHAT LEVEL AM I ABLE TO...
manage my money effectively?

	$^{***}_{**}$	$^{**}_{**}$	$^{**}_{*}$	$**$	$*$
▶ **I CAN work with numbers with ease**					
● think logically					
● add and subtract					
● multiply and divide					
● calculate simple and compound interest					
▶ **I CAN make everyday transactions**					
● make bank deposits and withdrawals					
● fill in cheques, statements, bills, etc.					
● reimburse payments and interest					
▶ **I CAN make different transactions**					
● take out an insurance policy					
– determine the nature of the insurance policy (life, disability, fire and theft, automobile, travel, liability, all risks)					
– verify the rate of the insurance premium, the clauses, the reimbursement					
● take out a mortgage and a bank loan					
– shop around for a bank and lending organization and interview them					

$^{***}_{**}$ = Excellent $^{**}_{**}$ = Very Good $^{**}_{*}$ = Good $**$ = Fair $*$ = None

	*** **	** **	** *	**	*
– check competitive rates					
– negotiate the best rate and ascertain the terms of the loan					
– supply guarantees (certificates, stocks, shares, etc.)					

▶ *I CAN negotiate stocks and shares*

	*** **	** **	** *	**	*
● interpret economic data					
● use the appropriate vocabulary (currency, stocks, bonds, options, indexes, balances, ratings, etc.)					
● follow the stock market, its indexes and trends					
● analyse a graph and interpret the curves					

*** ** = Excellent   ** ** = Very Good   ** * = Good   ** = Fair   * = None

AT WHAT LEVEL AM I ABLE TO...
manage my revenues and expenses and create a financial plan?

▶ *I CAN establish the state of my own and my family's income and expenses*

Income

- calculate my employment income (full or part-time work, contract work, etc.) and that of each family member contributing to the family budget
- calculate other income (commission, profits, bonuses, pensions, etc.)
- calculate family allowance income

***\n**	**\n**	**\n*	**	*

***\n** = Excellent   **\n** = Very Good   **\n* = Good   ** = Fair   * = None

	*** **	** **	** *	**	*
• calculate income from different sources (rent, interest, dividends, etc.)					
• calculate income resulting from the production of goods and services (prepared meals, sewing, knitting, weaving, crafts, odd jobs, child care, gardening, house cleaning, etc.)					
• anticipate new revenue					

Expenses

• calculate basic expenses (food, housing, electricity, heating, telephone, insurance, taxes, income tax, etc.)					
• calculate other expenses (clothing, furniture, medical and dental expenses, travel, day care, maintenance, help, cleaning, repairs, etc.)					
• calculate the allowances to pay for the children in my care					
• calculate expenses related to loans (mortgages, credit margins, etc.)					
• calculate miscellaneous expenses (leisure-time activities, holidays, gifts, long-term illness, etc.)					
• budget for unexpected expenses					

***
** = Excellent   **
** = Very Good   **
* = Good   ** = Fair   * = None

	*** **	** **	** *	**	*

▶ *I CAN plan my personal finances and my family's finances*

- seek out information from others (accountant, tax specialist, bank, consulting group, lending society, etc.)
  - find out about loans
- make a budget
  - establish and justify my priorities
  - anticipate necessary income
  - target unnecessary expenses
  - cut expenses in the appropriate places
  - predict additional money requirements
- request a loan
  - explain and justify my budget through examples and statistics
  - evaluate different ways to borrow money
- do my own and my family's bookkeeping

▶ *I CAN establish the income and expenses of a small business*

Income

- calculate revenue generated from professional services and the sale of goods
- calculate other revenues (grants, allowances, loans, etc.)

*** ** = Excellent   ** ** = Very Good   ** * = Good   ** = Fair   * = None

	Excellent	Very Good	Good	Fair	None
	***\n**	**\n**	**\n*	**	*
• calculate revenue from different sources (interest on loans, dividends, credits)					

Expenses

• calculate basic expenses (renting or purchasing a location for the business, taxes, equipment, electricity, heating, business telephone, insurance, stationary, etc.)					
• calculate expenses in professional fees, salaries, etc.					
• calculate other expenses (publicity and marketing, sales representation, travel, conferences, maintenance, etc.)					
• predict and calculate miscellaneous expenses (improvements to the locale, new equipment, vacations, etc.)					
• budget for unexpected expenses					

▶ ***I CAN plan the finances of a small business***

• seek out information from others (accountant, tax specialist, bank, consulting group, lending society, etc.)					
– find out about loans					
• make a budget					
– establish and justify my priorities					
– anticipate necessary revenues					
– target unnecessary expenses					

***/** = Excellent   **/** = Very Good   **/* = Good   ** = Fair   * = None

	*** **	** **	** *	**	*
– cut expenses in the appropriate places					
– predict additional money requirements					
● request a loan					
– explain and justify the budget through examples and statistics					
– evaluate different ways to borrow money					
● do the bookkeeping					
– for a salaried employee					
– for a contract worker					
– for a nonprofit organization					
– for an incorporated company					
● show the state of the company's revenues and expenses					
– verify the books and the accounts					
– keep the bankbooks up to date					
– prepare the books for auditing by the accountant					

*** ** = Excellent   ** ** = Very Good   ** * = Good   ** = Fair   * = None

Category 7

Planning and organizing

A single mother of four is planning her family's first camping expedition. She has received a lot of advice and encouragement from many of her friends who are supposedly well-seasoned campers. They have told her all about the joys of camping under the stars and communing with nature...

Wishing to avoid the unnecessary costs and disappointments that might result from her inexperience, the mother accepts her friends' offers to lend her the equipment she will need. By all appearances, her preparations are complete for her wilderness adventure—the only items left to add are food, water, and a few personal belongings.

The children are very enthusiastic about their upcoming adventure. The preparations go very well, that is, until the mother, who has always had a good deal of foresight, decides to inspect the borrowed equipment.

This is when she discovers to her dismay that the tent roof has a hole in it, in a perfect spot for letting in the rain drop by drop... And nothing seems to work when she tries to fix the folding table's wobbly legs. This table was supposed to help keep the food away from insects and other small four-legged visitors... And the large lantern that was supposed to be functional as well as decorative does not even work. The list of problems/repairs grows...

Faced with these problems, the mother decides to delegate tasks to each of her children. They help her not only to inspect the equipment, but to plan the camping adventure from A to Z. The mother wants to do everything she can to make this eagerly-anticipated expedition memorable, but for all the right reasons!

Definition

Competence in planning and organizing means having acquired knowledge and knowing what to do and how to be so that you can forecast and unite all the necessary elements to ensure the satisfactory execution of a project.

▶ DISCOVERING MY COMPETENCE IN PLANNING AND ORGANIZING

AT WHAT LEVEL AM I ABLE TO...
plan and organize effectively?

	$\overset{***}{**}$	$\overset{**}{**}$	$\overset{**}{*}$	**	*

▶ I CAN analyse a situation
- determine and evaluate the needs (what has to be done)
- take future needs into consideration
- prioritize the tasks to be accomplished

▶ I CAN create an action plan
- show creativity
- set a goal and objectives (visualize the results)
- imagine the steps required to reach the goal and the established objectives
- determine the activities and tasks to be accomplished
- determine the human and material resources required (money, equipment)
- make a work schedule

▶ I CAN put an action plan to work
- take initiative
- determine and gather together the human resources and required materials

$\overset{***}{**}$ = Excellent $\overset{**}{**}$ = Very Good $\overset{**}{*}$ = Good   ** = Fair   * = None

***** **	** **	** *	**	*

- respect the deadlines set
- re-evaluate the action plan frequently
- modify the action plan when necessary

AT WHAT LEVEL AM I ABLE TO...
plan and organize different activities?

***** **	** **	** *	**	*

▶ *I CAN plan and organize my personal life and that of my family*
- draw up a daily, monthly, yearly action plan
- make an inventory and analysis of each person's needs
- determine and divide up the duties and responsibilities (parents, partners, children, etc.)
- reconcile many different responsibilities (education, meals, care, travel, work, volunteer work, etc.)
- determine where to live – geographic location and type of dwelling (city, country; apartment, house, etc.)
- create and follow a budget (see the Financial Management section)

***** ** = Excellent   ** ** = Very Good   ** * = Good   ** = Fair   * = None

	*** **	** **	** *	**	*

- create and follow a schedule (work, study, leisure time, volunteer work, etc.)
- anticipate the unexpected

▶ *I CAN plan and organize family and social events*
- draw up an action plan
- establish the nature of the event and its objectives
- recognize the people involved and divide up the tasks and responsibilities among them
- determine the date and location of the event
- create a schedule and keep to it
- create a budget and keep to it (see the Financial Management section)
- reevaluate the action plan from time to time
- modify the action plan when necessary

▶ *I CAN plan and organize my own work and the work of a team, department, company*
- create a work or business plan
- establish the nature of my work
  - recognize the people involved (colleagues, bosses, subordinates, customers, suppliers, etc.)
  - determine the responsibilities of each person involved

***
** = Excellent   **
** = Very Good   **
* = Good   ** = Fair   * = None

Rate Yourself!

	*** **	** **	** *	**	*
• decide the place of work	___	___	___	___	___
• create a schedule and keep to it	___	___	___	___	___
• create a budget and keep to it	___	___	___	___	___
• prepare a work contract	___	___	___	___	___
– establish and guarantee the work schedule, pay, social benefits, vacation time, conditions for the termination of the contract and the cessation of the job, etc.					

Category 8

Problem solving

*T*he administration of a volunteer organization has called a meeting. The purpose of the meeting: to tackle a problem that is undermining the group's smooth operation. Something needs to be done right away because although the problem seems to be quite small now, it is in danger of growing.

For some time now, the pleasant, easy atmosphere that has always characterized the group's activities has been replaced by a quiet, more sombre mood. No one quite knows the reason why.

And yet by all outward signs, the organization is in the best shape ever. Just recently, the group moved to a new and brighter *location and received a donation of computer equipment. While the equipment is a little dated, it can provide exactly the type of computer support the group requires. As a result, the organization is able to perform a number of tasks more efficiently than before. New people have joined the group. These new additions cannot be the problem because all were selected with the approval of every member of the administrative committee.*

There had been some concern within the administration that the group's grant would be cut this year, but the fears proved unfounded. Recognizing the organization's indispensable contribution to the community, the government easily renewed the grant for another year.

It seems, then, that everything is in place to ensure that the organization continues to provide its services while maintaining an agreeable work environment. But still the uneasiness remains... Perhaps the offices need to be redecorated. Perhaps the air quality of the building needs to be checked. Are some of the volunteers overworked? Stressed out? The furtive nods and whispers continue, the unexplained absences persist... Clearly people within the organization are not as happy as they once were and there is no obvious reason why... Or could it be that no one dares to say?

What problem does the volunteer organization have and what solution must be found?

Definition

Competence in problem solving means having acquired knowledge and knowing what to do and how to be so that you can clearly grasp a problem and find realistic and applicable solutions.

▶ DISCOVERING MY COMPETENCE IN PROBLEM SOLVING

AT WHAT LEVEL AM I ABLE TO...
solve a problem effectively?

	*** **	** **	** *	**	*
▶ *I CAN accept that there is a problem*					
● not panic					
● give myself time to think about it					
● have confidence in myself and keep a positive outlook					
▶ *I CAN think logically*					
● show objectivity					
● focus on the problem					
▶ *I CAN move into action*					
● give free rein to my imagination					
● explore different possible solutions					
● choose the best solution					

***
** = Excellent   **
** = Very Good   **
* = Good   ** = Fair   * = None

AT WHAT LEVEL AM I ABLE TO...
solve different kinds of problems?

	*** **	** **	** *	**	*
▶ **I CAN observe and describe the nature of the problem**					
• observe and explain a problem with things (broken object, defective plumbing, etc.)					
• observe and explain a financial problem (unbalanced budget, the refusal of a mortgage loan, etc.)					
• observe and explain a social or human problem (a breakdown in communication, delinquent behaviour, etc.)					

***
** = Excellent   **
** = Very Good   **
* = Good   ** = Fair   * = None

	*** **	** **	** *	**	*

- observe and explain an artistic or aesthetic problem (poorly coordinated clothing, clashing decorating scheme, unpleasant noises, etc.)
- observe and explain a conceptual or intellectual problem (lack of strategic planning, etc.)

▶ *I CAN analyse, understand and evaluate the problem*
- think logically
- verify my understanding
- differentiate between essential and less important elements
- use my creativity to find solutions .
- evaluate and compare the advantages and disadvantages of each solution

▶ *I CAN choose the best solution and put it into action*
- evaluate and judge the best solution
- eliminate the other options
- take risks
- accept that the solution may not be agreeable to everyone
- put into practice what I have imagined

*** ** = Excellent   ** ** = Very Good   ** * = Good   ** = Fair   * = None

	*** **	** **	** *	**	*

▶ *I CAN ensure a follow-up and fine-tuning of my method*
- verify how the chosen approach is applied
- modify my action plan if necessary or even reject the chosen solution if it does not prove effective
- persevere and show flexibility

Category 9

Entrepreneurship

*N*ews of the inaugural festivities has made Page One of all the local papers!

This is how it all began... A house left unoccupied by the death of its owner some years back is in a sorry state of disrepair – windows are broken, slates are missing from the roof, and the entire exterior needs several coats of paint. The neighbourhood children are convinced the house is haunted...

The house stands in this dilapidated condition because of a dispute among the inheritors. Finally, the case is resolved in court and the house is immediately put up for sale. The price is extremely reasonable because of the neglected state of the property.

Five friends who are currently unemployed eye the property with a good deal of interest and get together to discuss the possibilities. Using their imaginations to see past the bad state the house is presently in, they all agree that with a bit of capital, they could renovate the house and set up a small and budding business there—perhaps even several small businesses.

Each of the friends can bring particular talents and abilities to the project. One woman is eager to tackle the renovations, using her expertise in this area. She is not in the least bit afraid of the ghosts that apparently occupy the building.

Another friend is anxious to use the financial management and sales expertise she developed as the owner of a clothing boutique. She had to sell the boutique when the lease expired on the premises. She suggests opening a nearly-new clothing shop on the premises.

There is a couple in the group that had at one time operated a small and successful café/restaurant. At their café/restaurant, they cooked up tasty meals for their hurried customers in a very short time. The customers always marvelled at their talent.

The last member of the group would like to set up an employment service for people looking for work. This person has had to change jobs herself fairly frequently in the past and would like to share what she has learned with others. An enthusiastic amateur botanist, this final member of the group would also like to cultivate plants to sell in a small florist's shop on the premises.

Everyone agrees that there is a good deal of talent in the group. Together they see that the neglected old home can have a new life as nothing less than a multi-service centre!

Four months later, news of the building's reopening is in all the papers. To take part in the opening-day festivities, visitors must bring along one of the following items: an advertisement for a job that needs to be filled, a fine home-cooked meal, a decorative houseplant, or an article of clothing to donate. The festivities turn out to be a great success, and thankfully, no ghosts or disgruntled inheritors were in attendance!

Definition

Competence in entrepreneurship means having acquired knowledge and knowing what to do and how to be so that with perhaps very little money or resources, you are able to start your own business, either on your own or with others.

▶ DISCOVERING MY COMPETENCE IN ENTREPRENEURSHIP

AT WHAT LEVEL AM I ABLE TO...
bring together the favourable conditions for creating a
small business?

	*** **	** **	** *	**	*
▶ **I CAN put my basic skills and abilities to good use (see the preceding categories)**					
● communicate					
– verbally and nonverbally					
● read					
● write					
● establish interpersonal relations					
● use a computer at work					
● manage a budget					
● plan and organize					
● solve problems					
▶ **I CAN persevere with a project**					
● use the energy required					
● have confidence in myself					
● overcome uncertainty and stress					
▶ **I CAN take calculated risks**					
● accept a challenge without fear					
● accept and evaluate my ability to live without a steady income from time to time					

***
** = Excellent   **
** = Very Good   **
* = Good   ** = Fair   * = None

*** **	** **	** *	**	*

- take on realistic loans and repay them
- verify my ability to work for myself or with associates
- understand the implications my involvement in a small business will have for my personal and professional life

AT WHAT LEVEL AM I ABLE TO...
start up and run a small business?

*** **	** **	** *	**	*

▶ *I CAN create a business plan*
- visualize a project, a concept (products and services)
- seek out information (through consultations, books, leaflets, specialized magazines, courses, workshops, seminars, etc.)
- make a study of the market (assess how realistic the project is, the demand for this type of product or service)
- establish the type of business it will be
- determine the human resources required (to hire, contract out, etc.)
- determine the material resources required (office space, equipment, furniture, stationery, telephones, fax machines, computers, etc.)

*** ** = Excellent   ** ** = Very Good   ** * = Good   ** = Fair   * = None

	*** **	** **	** *	**	*
• develop a marketing plan (initial marketing of the product or service)					
• establish a calendar of activities (schedule)					
▶ I CAN take out loans					
• survey all the lending establishments					
• submit my business plan					
• explain the validity of my business					
• supply loan guarantees					
• legally establish the company					
• make commitments and keep to them					
▶ I CAN create a network					
• join associations and business groups					
• participate in seminars, workshops, training courses					
• consult with others who are competent in the field when necessary					

***
** = Excellent   **
** = Very Good   **
* = Good   ** = Fair   * = None

Category 10

Special category: my personality traits

*W*e all find ourselves looking for a competent individual at some point or other. But the truth is that know-how alone does not make a person competent. Ask yourself this question: How can an employee hired because of his or her knowledge demand and get twice the usual fee for his or her work? Or how can it be that an employee provides a service or product that is decidedly inferior to what was expected? The employee's personality traits probably have a lot to do with it. They can heighten or diminish the person's competence.

We associate with competence certain specific principles and merit. A person in possession of these qualities is a much more attractive individual than one without them. That is what makes us choose one person over another even though two individuals have developed their skills and abilities in the same field at the same academic institution, etc.

Of course, a person's competence can be influenced by any number factors, including the circumstances of her life and her upbringing. It goes without saying that certain personality traits are often revealed at the time a person is recruited and hired. These personality traits can make the person an even more desirable candidate, but then again, they can also do just the opposite.

To discover the principal characteristics expected of a competent person, ask yourself the following questions: Would you be satisfied with a person lacking initiative? With a person who refuses to continue to learn and evolve? With a person who rants and raves about his pseudoscientific theories at every possible opportunity? What would you think of an electrician who does an excellent job repairing the wiring in your home, but has a horrible manner? What would you think of a loved one who betrays you? And if there ever comes a day when you must explain to a judge that someone has stolen your car and your goods, how would you feel if the judge lacked objectivity?

What makes a person competent?

Definition

The personality traits focussed on here are a combination of acquired knowledge and knowing how to do, but most especially how to be that distinguish you from all others and add to your competence.

▶ *DISCOVERING MY PERSONALITY TRAITS*

	*** **	** **	** *	**	*

▶ *Am I efficient and conscientious?*
I AM ABLE TO
- interpret instructions, orders
- work within normal deadlines
- have initiative

▶ *Am I adaptable?*
I AM ABLE TO
- be open to change when necessary
- learn day by day
- evolve when necessary

▶ *Am I objective?*
I AM ABLE TO
- focus on the objectives and the people
- make reliable judgments
- be self-critical

▶ *Am I honest?*
I AM ABLE TO
- distinguish between good and evil
- reject negative influences
- be ethical and moral

*** ** = Excellent   ** ** = Very Good   ** * = Good   ** = Fair   * = None

	*** **	** **	** *	**	*

▶ *Am I responsible?*
I AM ABLE TO
- make and keep commitments
- complete a task
- explain the reasons behind my actions

▶ *Am I loyal and trustworthy?*
I AM ABLE TO
- be loyal to others
- be loyal to my commitments
- be loyal to my principles

▶ *Am I courageous?*
I AM ABLE TO
- take risks
- defend my ideas, opinions, rights
- work for a cause I believe in

▶ *Am I able to speak intelligently about different subjects?*
I AM ABLE TO
- talk about subjects in many different fields, drawing on my personal knowledge
- comment on certain facts by referring to concrete data
- comment on subjects in different domains and make objective criticisms

*** ** = Excellent   ** ** = Very Good   ** * = Good   ** = Fair   * = None

80

	*** **	** **	** *	**	*

▶ *Am I intuitive?*
I AM ABLE TO
- guess and predict needs, events, things
- anticipate the actions that must be taken
- predict trends in intellectual thought

▶ *Am I stable?*
I AM ABLE TO
- control my emotions
- think before making decisions
- give myself time to relax

▶ *Am I sensitive to moral/ethical issues?*
I AM ABLE TO
- sensitize myself to current social and environmental issues
- explain the nature of these issues
- take a position with respect to these issues

▶ *Am I humane?*
I AM ABLE TO
- love
- be pleasant to others
- listen to others

***
** = Excellent   **
** = Very Good   **
* = Good   ** = Fair   * = None

Summary

*A*s was mentioned in the very beginning, the principal objective of this book is to allow you to **name** your transferable skills and abilities as well as your personality traits and **classify** them into categories.

Now that you have completed the 10 questionnaires, you have a clear idea of the many skills you have developed during the course of your life. The next step is for you to get a global view of the areas where your strengths lie as well as the areas where you are not as strong. The following summary questionnaire will help you to do this.

The questionnaire lists the major questions explored in the 10 questionnaires. Write down the rating you most often gave yourself for each major category. For example, if within a given category you most often answered 'Good,' then write 'Good' in the summary questionnaire as well.

Category 1 – Communication (verbal and nonverbal communication, reading, writing)

	$*{*}^{*}_{**}$	$*{*}_{**}$	$*{*}_{*}$	**	*
▶ **DISCOVERING MY VERBAL AND NONVERBAL COMMUNICATION SKILLS, MY READING SKILLS, MY WRITING SKILLS AT WHAT LEVEL AM I ABLE TO...**					
• Communicate effectively?					
• Communicate in public?					
• Read effectively?					
• Read different types of material on different subjects?					
• Write effectively?					
• Write in different styles?					

Category 2 – Interpersonal relations

	$*{*}^{*}_{**}$	$*{*}_{**}$	$*{*}_{*}$	**	*
▶ **DISCOVERING MY COMPETENCE IN INTERPERSONAL RELATIONS AT WHAT LEVEL AM I ABLE TO...**					
• Develop and maintain good and effective interpersonal relations?					
• Develop and maintain interpersonal relations at work and in social and community activities?					
• Develop and maintain interpersonal relations when I am in a leadership role?					

*** = Excellent   ** = Very Good   ** = Good   ** = Fair   * = None

84

Category 3 – Computer skills

*** **	** **	** *	**	*

▶ *DISCOVERING MY COMPETENCE WITH COMPUTERS*
AT WHAT LEVEL AM I ABLE TO...
- Use computers effectively on the job?
- Master different ways of using computers?

Category 4 – Physical abilities and manual skills

*** **	** **	** *	**	*

▶ *DISCOVERING MY PHYSICAL ABILITIES AND MANUAL SKILLS*
AT WHAT LEVEL AM I ABLE TO...
- Make effective movements and gestures?
- Make effective movements and gestures in different types of activities?
- Effectively demonstrate my manual skills?
- Demonstrate my manual skills in different contexts?

***
** = Excellent   **
** = Very Good   **
* = Good   ** = Fair   * = None

85

Category 5 – Artistic expression

	*** **	** **	** *	**	*

▶ *DISCOVERING MY*
COMPETENCE IN ARTISTIC
EXPRESSION
AT WHAT LEVEL AM I ABLE TO...
- Use my artistic talents effectively?
- Use my artistic talents in different activities that involve one of the five senses?

Category 6 – Financial management

	*** **	** **	** *	**	*

▶ *DISCOVERING MY*
COMPETENCE IN FINANCIAL
MANAGEMENT
AT WHAT LEVEL AM I ABLE TO...
- Manage my money effectively?
- Manage my revenues and expenses and create a financial plan?

Category 7 – Planning and organizing

	*** **	** **	** *	**	*

▶ *DISCOVERING MY*
COMPETENCE IN PLANNING
AND ORGANIZING
AT WHAT LEVEL AM I ABLE
TO...
- Plan and organize effectively?
- Plan and organize different activities?

*** ** = Excellent   ** ** = Very Good   ** * = Good   ** = Fair   * = None

Category 8 – Problem solving

*** **	** **	** *	**	*

▶ *DISCOVERING MY*
COMPETENCE IN PROBLEM
SOLVING
AT WHAT LEVEL AM I ABLE
TO...
- Solve a problem effectively?
- Solve different kinds of problems?

Category 9 – Entrepreneurship

*** **	** **	** *	**	*

▶ *DISCOVERING MY*
COMPETENCE IN
ENTREPRENEURSHIP
AT WHAT LEVEL AM I ABLE
TO...
- Bring together the favourable
  conditions for creating a small
  business?
- Start up and run a small business?

*** = Excellent ** = Very Good ** = Good ** = Fair * = None
 **   **   *

Category 10 – Special category: my personality traits

	*** **	** **	** *	**	*

▶ *DISCOVERING MY PERSONALITY TRAITS AM I...*
- Efficient and conscientious?
- Adaptable?
- Objective?
- Honest?
- Responsible?
- Loyal and trustworthy?
- Courageous?
- Able to speak intelligently about different subjects?
- Intuitive?
- Stable?
- Sensitive to moral/ethical issues?
- Humane?

*** ** = Excellent   ** ** = Very Good   ** * = Good   ** = Fair   * = None

Congratulations!

Now that you have completed your summary questionnaire, the time has come to share your newly-discovered potential with prospective employers. For example, in a letter requesting employment, you could list by order of importance the principal categories in which you can place your competence: verbal and nonverbal communication, reading, writing, interpersonal relations, computer skills, physical abilities and manual skills, artistic expression, financial management, planning and organizing, problem solving, entrepreneurship and personality traits.

When you write your CV, you can mention your principal skills and abilities and your personality traits immediately after you list your education and employment history.

In job application forms, there is often space provided for your comments. You can use this space to list your principal skills and abilities.

If you are creating a portfolio with the intention of requesting recognition of your prior learning in order to return to school or work, there are a number of places in the portfolio where you can describe your skills and competencies. You can mention them, for example, when you write your autobiography, your training objectives, and when you identify your prior learning (in such areas as credit courses, non-credit courses, paid work, unpaid work (volunteer work, for example), leisure, travel and sports activities, etc.).

It is very possible that you will be going to a job interview in the near future. The simple fact that you have completed the questionnaires should jog your memory and help you to answer some of the questions you will be asked.

Whatever way you use the information about yourself that you have gathered from this book, remember to always remain confident in yourself!

And may you have great success!